Impressum
Verlag: BABADADA GmbH, Nedderfeld 112 , 22529 Hamburg
Geschäftsführer / Verlagsleitung: Harald Hof
Druck: Books on Demand GmbH, In de Tarpen 42, 22848 Norderstedt

Imprint
Publisher: BABADADA GmbH, Nedderfeld 112 , 22529 Hamburg, Germany
Managing Director / Publishing direction: Harald Hof
Print: Books on Demand GmbH, In de Tarpen 42, 22848 Norderstedt

School

school

Klassenstuuv
classroom

delen
divide

186/2

Tafel
board

Schoolhoff
school yard

Schoolmeester
teacher

Papeer
paper

schrieven
write

Sticken
pen

Schrievdisch
desk

Lienholt
ruler

Book
book

Schöler
pupil

Ranzel

satchel

Feddermapp

pencil case

Bleesticken

pencil

Scharpmaker

pencil sharpener

Radeergummi

rubber

Tekenblock

drawing pad

Teken

drawing

Pinsel

paintbrush

Malkassen

paint box

Scheer

scissors

Klever

glue

Heft to'n Öven

exercise book

Huusopgaav

homework

Tall

number

tohooptellen

add

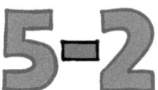

aftrecken

subtract

malnehmen

multiply

reken

calculate

Bookstaav

letter

ABC

alphabet

Woort

word

Text

text

lesen

read

Kried

chalk

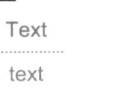

Stunn

lesson

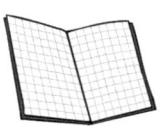

Klassenbook

register

Pröven

exam

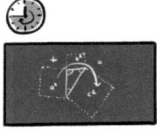

Tüügnis

certificate

Schooluniform

school uniform

Utbillen

education

Nakieksel

encyclopedia

Universität

university

Mikroskop

microscope

Koort

map

Papeerkorf

waste-paper basket

Törn
travel

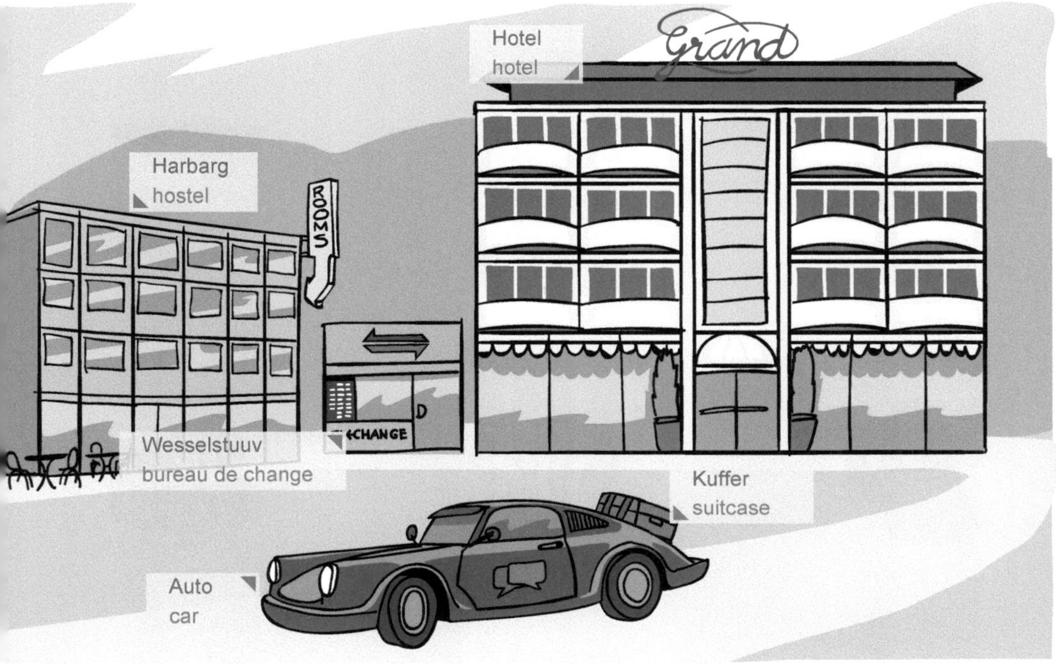
Hotel
hotel
Grand
Harbarg
hostel
ROOMS
CHANGE
Wesselstuuv
bureau de change
Kuffer
suitcase
Auto
car

Spraak

language

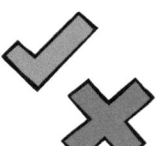

jo / ne

yes / no

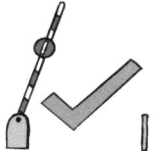

Jo

Okay

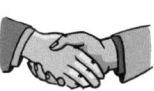

Moin

hello

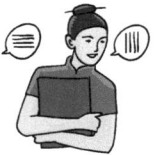

Översetter

translator

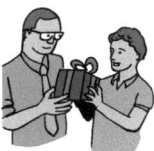

Dank ok

Thank you

Wat kost...?

how much is...?

Ik verstah nich

I do not understand

Problem

problem

Goden Avend

Good evening!

Moin!

Good morning!

Gode Nacht!

Good night!

Tschüüs

bye bye

Richt

direction

Bagaasch

luggage

Tasch

bag

Rüchsack

backpack

Gast

guest

Stuuv

room

Slaapsack

sleeping bag

Telt

tent

Touristeninformatschoon

tourist information

Strand

beach

Kreditkoort

credit card

Fröhstück

breakfast

Meddageten

lunch

Avendeten

dinner

Fohrkort

ticket

Fohrstohl

lift

Breefmark

stamp

Grenz

border

Toll

customs

Bottschop

embassy

Visum

visa

Pass

passport

Transport
transport

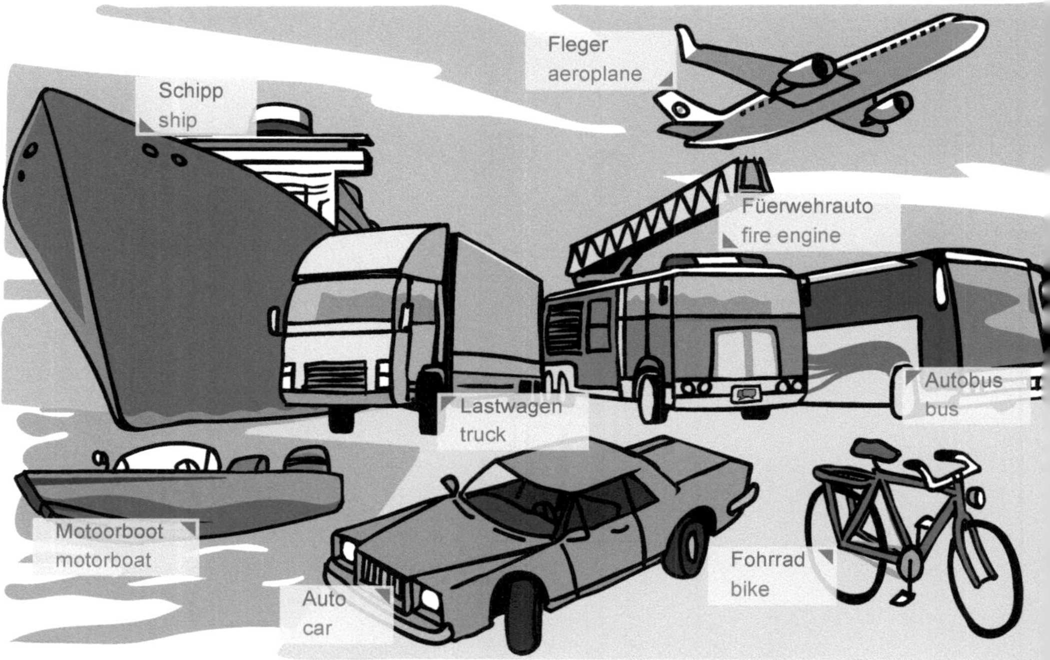
Fleger
aeroplane
Schipp
ship
Füerwehrauto
fire engine
Lastwagen
truck
Autobus
bus
Motoorboot
motorboat
Fohrrad
bike
Auto
car

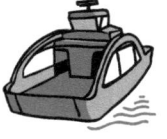

Fähr

ferry

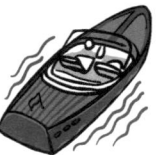

Boot

boat

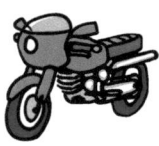

Motoorrad

motorbike

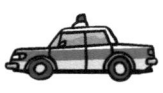

Polizeiauto

police car

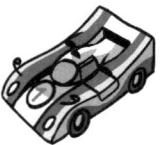

Rönnauto

racing car

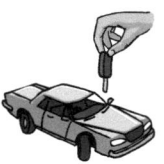

Lehnwagen

rental car

Carsharing

car sharing

Afsleepwagen

breakdown truck

Müllauto

refuse truck

Motoor

motor

Kraftstoff

fuel

Tanksteed

petrol station

Verkehrsschild

traffic sign

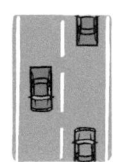

Verkehr

traffic

Stau

traffic jam

Afstellplatz

car park

Bahnhoff

train station

Sporen

tracks

Tog

train

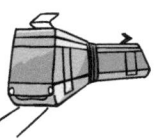

Stratenbahn

tram

Wagon

carriage

Dwarsmöhl

helicopter

Flooghaven

airport

Tower

tower

Fohrgast

passenger

Grootkist

container

Karton

carton

Koor

cart

Korf

basket

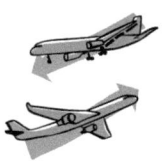

starten / lannen

take off / land

Stadt
city

Dörp

village

Binnenstadt

city centre

Huus

house

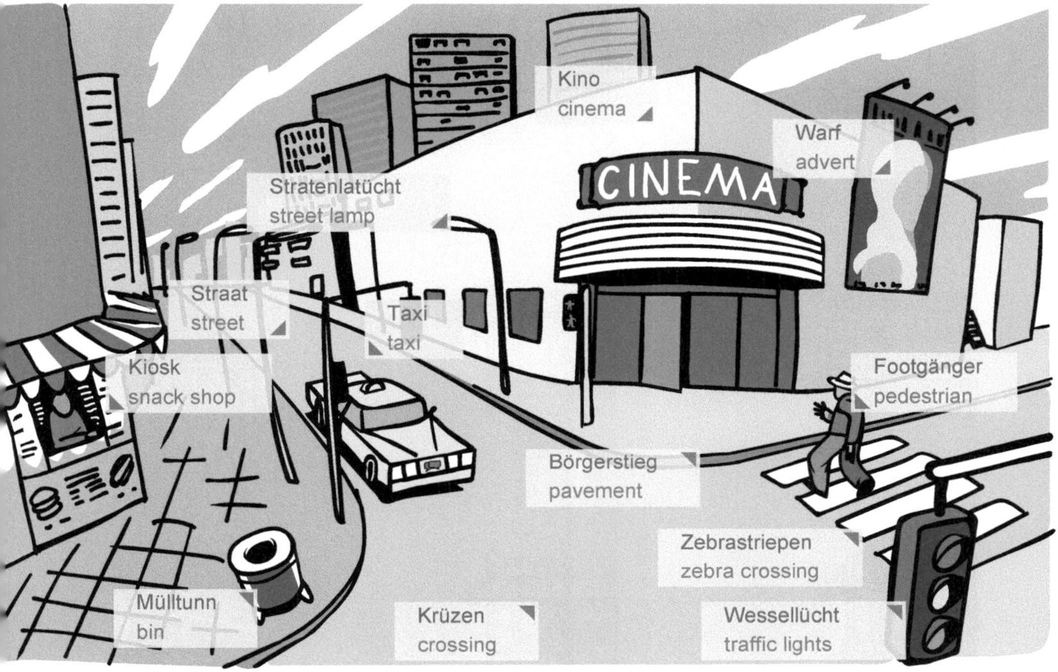

Kino
cinema

Warf
advert

Stratenlatücht
street lamp

CINEMA

Straat
street

Taxi
taxi

Footgänger
pedestrian

Kiosk
snack shop

Börgerstieg
pavement

Zebrastriepen
zebra crossing

Mülltunn
bin

Krüzen
crossing

Wessellücht
traffic lights

Hütt

hut

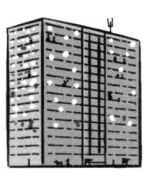

Wahnung

flat

Bahnhoff

train station

Raathuus

town hall

Museum

museum

School

school

Stadt - city

Universität

university

Bank

bank

Krankenhuus

hospital

Hotel

hotel

Afteek

pharmacy

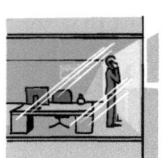

Büro

office

Bookhökerie

book shop

Hökerie

shop

Blomenhökerie

florist's

Supermarkt

supermarket

Markt

market

Koophuus

department store

Fischhökerie

fishmonger's

Inkoopszentrum

shopping centre

Haven

harbour

Parkanlaag

park

Bank

bench

Brüch

bridge

Trepp

stairs

Ünnergrundbahn

underground

Tunnel

tunnel

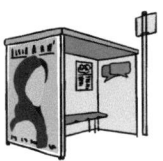

Busstoppsteed

bus stop

Bar

bar

Spieslokal

restaurant

Breefkassen

postbox

Stratenschild

street sign

Parkklock

parking meter

Deertenpark

zoo

Baadanstalt

swimming pool

Moschee

mosque

Buernhoff

farm

Ümweltversmudden

pollution

Karkhoff

graveyard

Kark

church

Speelplatz

playground

Tempel

temple

Landschop

landscape

Blatt
leaf

Wiespahl
signpost

Weg
way

Wisch
meadow

Steen
stone

Wannerer
hiker

Boom
tree

Fluss
river

Gras
grass

Bloom
flower

Daal

valley

Barg

hill

See

lake

Holt

forest

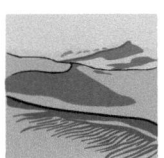

Wööst

desert

Füerspien Barg

volcano

Slott

castle

Regenbagen

rainbow

Poggenstohl

mushroom

Palm

palm tree

Steekmück

mosquito

Fleeg

fly

Miegeemk

ant

Imm

bee

Spinn

spider

Landschop - landscape

Sebber

beetle

Pogg

frog

Katteker

squirrel

Swienegel

hedgehog

Haas

hare

Uul

owl

Vagel

bird

Swaan

swan

Wildswien

boar

Hirsch

deer

Elk

moose

Staudamm

dam

Windrad

wind turbine

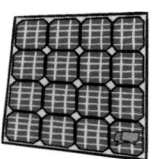

Solarmodul

solar panel

Klima

climate

Spieslokal
restaurant

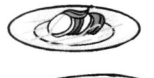

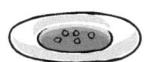

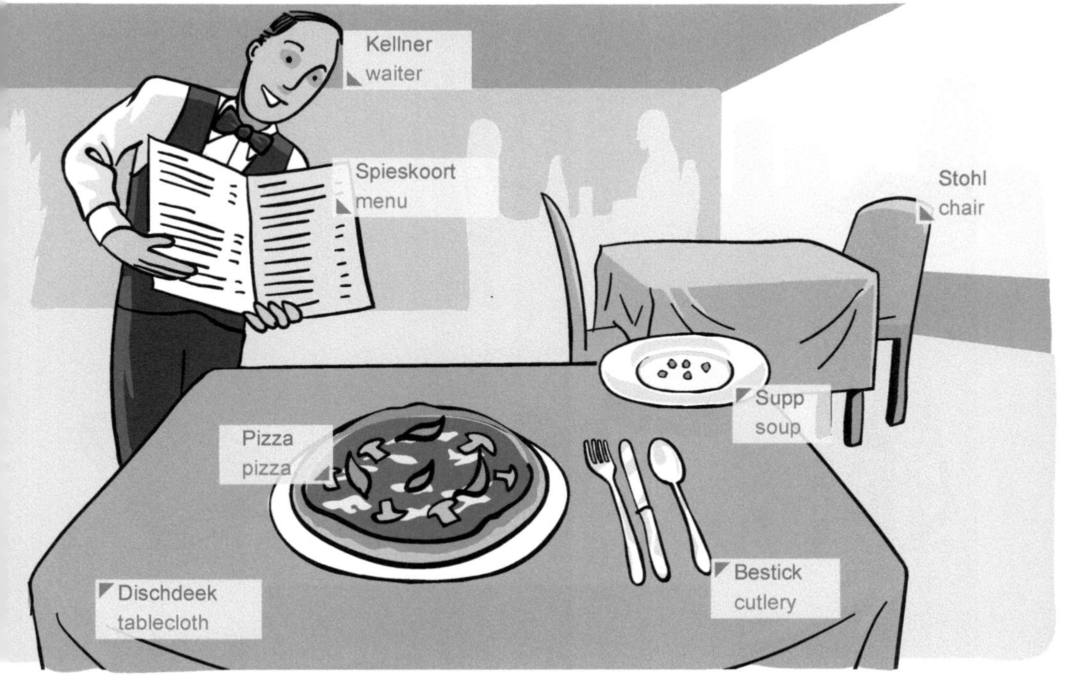
Kellner
waiter
Spieskoort
menu
Stohl
chair
Supp
soup
Pizza
pizza
Bestick
cutlery
Dischdeek
tablecloth

Vörspies

starter

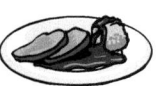

Haupteten

main course

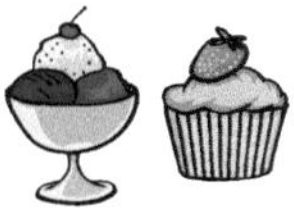

Nadisch

dessert

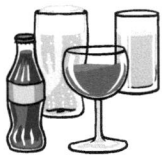

Drünk

drinks

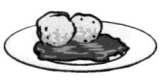

Eten

food

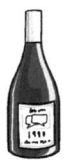

Buddel

bottle

Fastfood

fast food

Strateneten

street food

Teekann

teapot

Zuckerdoos

sugar bowl

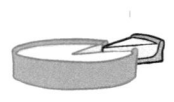

Portschoon

portion

Espressomaschien

espresso machine

Hoochstohl

high chair

Reken

bill

Tablett

tray

Mess

knife

Gavel

fork

Lepel

spoon

Teelepel

teaspoon

Munddook

serviette

Glas

glass

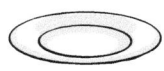

Töller

plate

Suppentöller

soup plate

Ünnertass

saucer

Sooß

sauce

Soltstreuer

salt pot

Pepermöhl

pepper mill

Etig

vinegar

Ööl

oil

Krüder

spices

Ketchup

ketchup

Mostrich

mustard

Mayonnaise

mayonnaise

Supermarkt

supermarket

Anbott
special offer
FOR
Kunn
customer
Melkprodukten
dairy
Aaft
fruit
Inkoopswagen
trolley

BUTCHERS

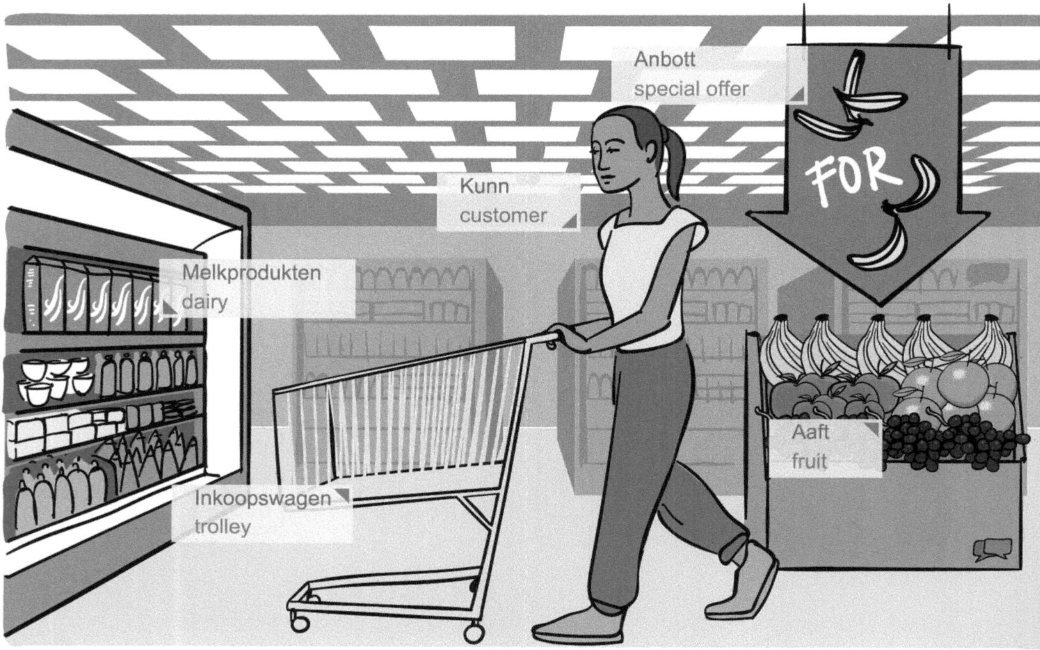

Slachterie

butcher´s

BAKERY

Bäckerie

baker´s

wegen

weigh

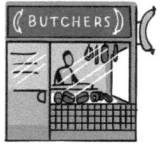

Gröönsaken

vegetables

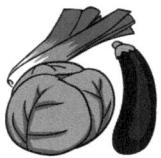

Fleesch

meat

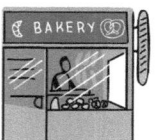

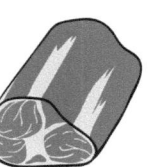

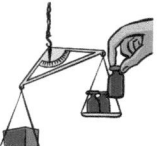

Deepköhlkost

frozen food

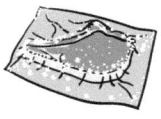

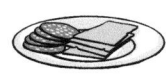

Opsnitt

cold meat

Konserven

tinned food

Waschmiddel

washing powder

Snoopkraam

sweets

Huushooltssaken

household products

Reinmaaktüüch

cleaning products

Verköpersche

salesperson

Kass

till

Kasserer

cashier

Inkoopslist

shopping list

Opsparrtieden

opening hours

Breeftasch

wallet

Kreditkoort

credit card

Tasch

bag

Plastiktüüt

plastic bag

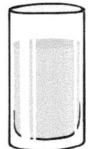

Water

water

Saft

juice

Melk

milk

Cola

coke

Wien

wine

Beer

beer

Spriet

alcohol

Kakao

cocoa

Tee

tea

Koffie

coffee

Espresso

espresso

Cappucino

cappuccino

Banaan

banana

Appel

apple

Appelsien

orange

Meloon

melon

Zitroon

lemon

Wöttel

carrot

Knuuvlook

garlic

Bambus

bamboo

Zibbel

onion

Poggenstohl

mushroom

Nööt

nuts

Nudeln

noodles

Spaghetti

spaghetti

Ries

rice

Salat

salad

Pommes frites

chips

Braadkantüffeln

fried potatoes

Pizza

pizza

Hamborger

hamburger

Sandwich

sandwich

Snitzel

cutlet

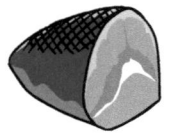

Schinken

ham

Salami

salami

Wust

sausage

Hohn

chicken

Braden

roast

Fisch

fish

Haverflocken

porridge oats

Müsli

muesli

Cornflakes

cornflakes

Mehl

flour

Croissant

croissant

Rundstück

bread roll

Broot

bread

Toast

toast

Keksen

biscuits

Botter

butter

Quark

curd

Koken

cake

Ei

egg

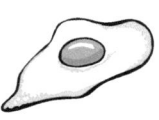

Spegelei

fried egg

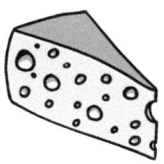

Kees

cheese

Ies
ice cream

Zucker
sugar

Honnig
honey

Marmelaad
jam

Nougat-Creme
chocolate spread

Curry
curry

Buernhoff

farm

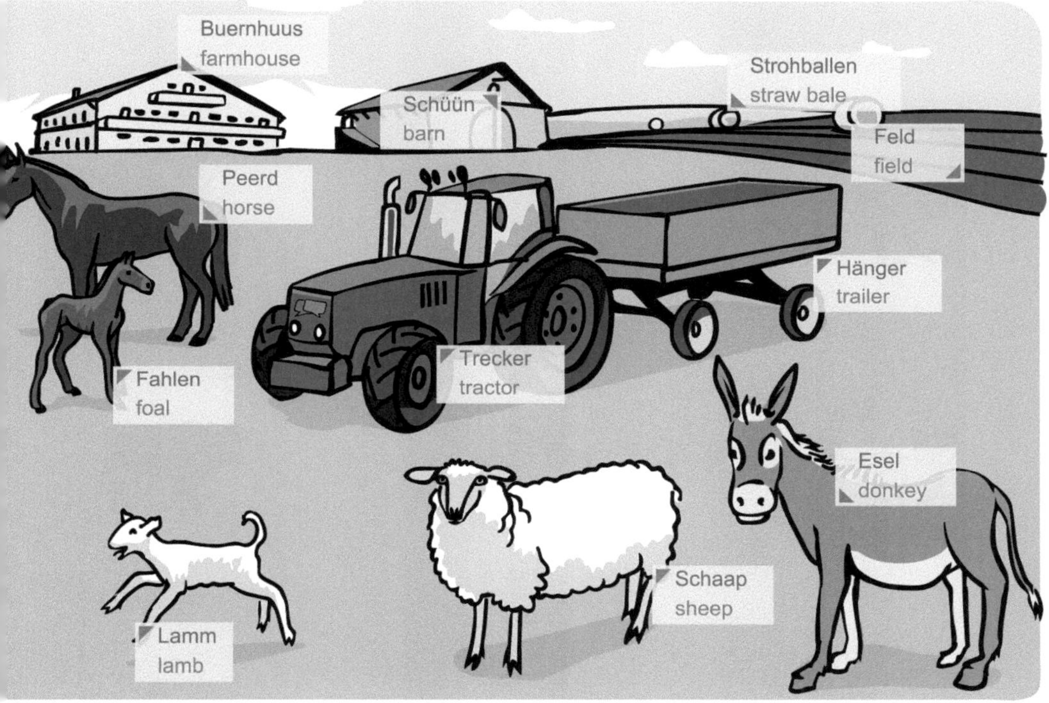
Buernhuus
farmhouse
Schüün
barn
Strohballen
straw bale
Feld
field
Peerd
horse
Hänger
trailer
Trecker
tractor
Fahlen
foal
Esel
donkey
Schaap
sheep
Lamm
lamb

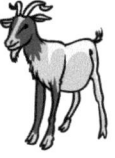

Zeeg

goat

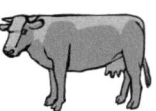

Koh

cow

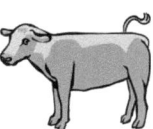

Kalf

calf

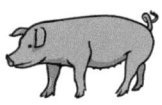

Swien

pig

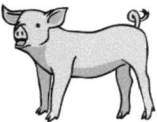

Farken

piglet

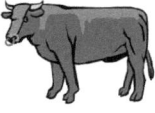

Bull

bull

Goos

goose

Aant

duck

Küken

chick

Hohn

hen

Hahn

cock

Rott

rat

Katt

cat

Muus

mouse

Oss

ox

Hund

dog

Hunnenhütt

doghouse

Goornslauch

garden hose

Geetkann

watering can

Lee

scythe

Ploog

plough

Sich

sickle

Hack

hoe

Mestfork

pitchfork

Ext

axe

Schuufkoor

wheelbarrow

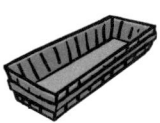

Trog

trough

Melkkann

milk can

Sack

sack

Tuun

fence

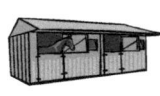

Stall

stable

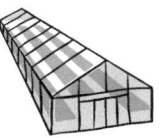

Drievhuus

greenhouse

Bodden

soil

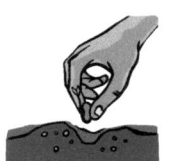

Saat

seed

Dünger

fertilizer

Meihdöscher

combine harvester

oornen

harvest

Oorn

harvest

Yamswöttel

yams

Weten

wheat

Soja

soy

Kantüffel

potato

Törksche Weten

corn

Rapp

rapeseed

Aaftboom

fruit tree

Troopsch Kantüffel

cassava

Koorn

cereals

Huus

house

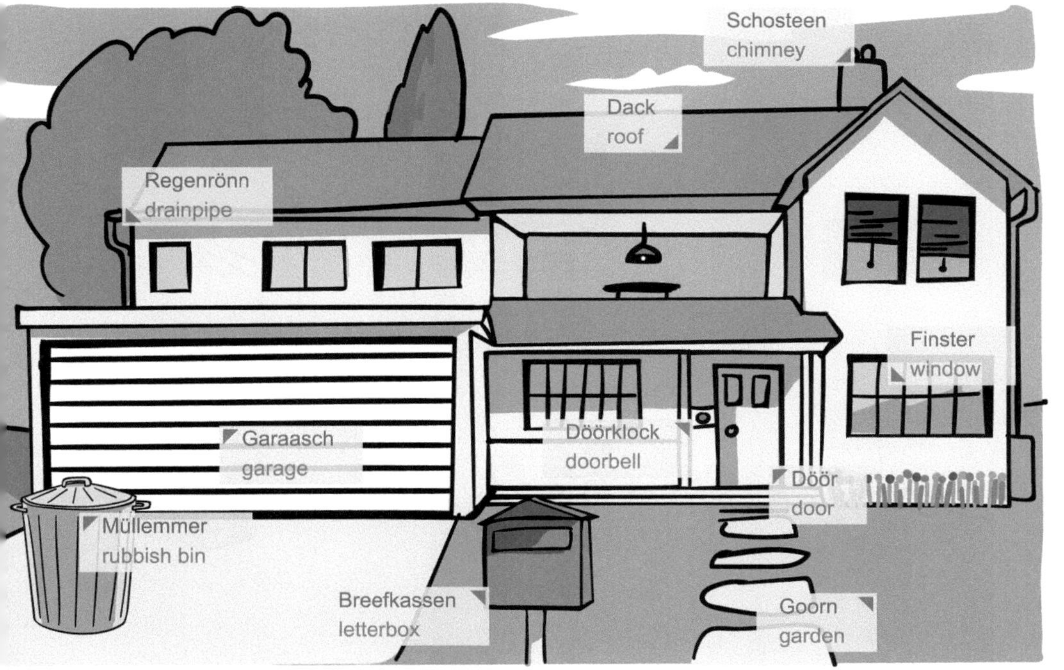

Schosteen
chimney
Dack
roof
Regenrönn
drainpipe
Finster
window
Garaasch
garage
Döörklock
doorbell
Döör
door
Müllemmer
rubbish bin
Breefkassen
letterbox
Goorn
garden

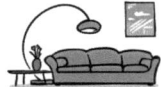

Wahnstuuv

living room

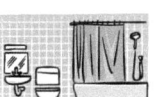

Baadstuuv

bathroom

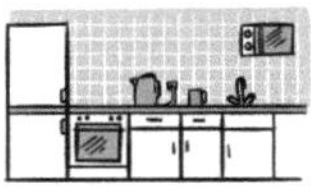

Köök

kitchen

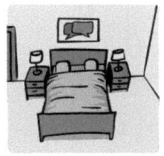

Slaapstuuv

bedroom

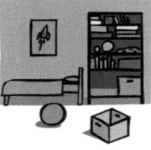

Kinnerstuuv

child's room

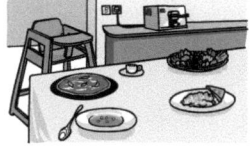

Eetstuuv

dining room

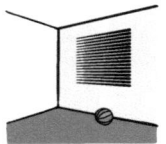

Footbodden

floor

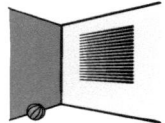

Wand

wall

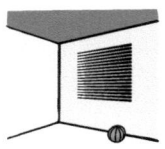

Deek

ceiling

Keller

cellar

Hittluftbad

sauna

Balkon

balcony

Terrass

terrace

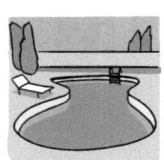

Swümmbad

pool

Rasenmeiher

lawn mower

Bettbetog

sheet

Bettdeek

bedspread

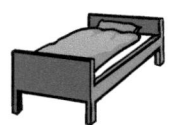

Puuch

bed

Bessen

broom

Emmer

bucket

Schalter

switch

Wahnstuuv

living room

Tapeet
wallpaper
Bild
picture
Lamp
lamp
Regal
shelf
Schapp
cupboard
Kiekkassen
television
Kamin
fireplace
Bloom
flower
Küssen
cushion
Sofa
sofa
Vaas
vase
Feernbedenen
remote control

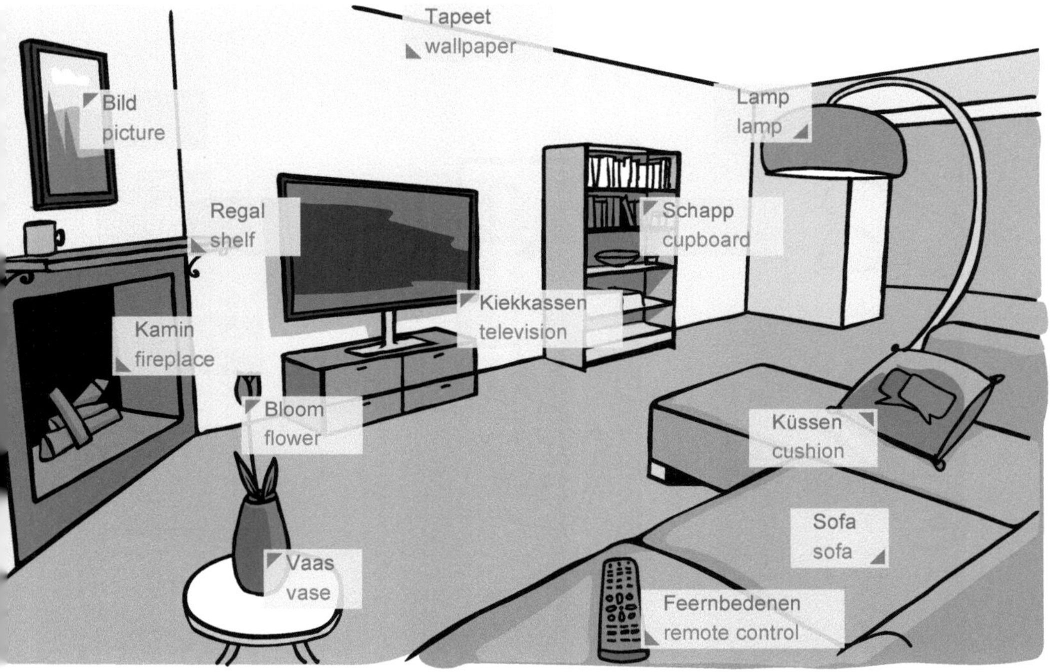

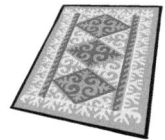

Teppich

carpet

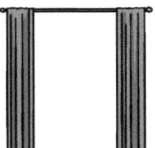

Vörhang

curtain

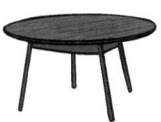

Disch

table

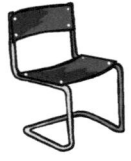

Stohl

chair

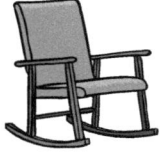

Schuckelstohl

rocking chair

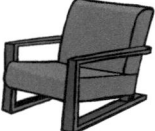

Sessel

armchair

Book
book

Deek
blanket

Dekoratschoon
decoration

Füerholt
firewood

Film
film

Stereoanlaag
hi-fi equipment

Slötel
key

Narichtenblatt
newspaper

Gemälde
painting

Poster
poster

Radio
radio

Opschrievblock
notepad

Huulbessen
hoover

Kaktus
cactus

Kars
candle

Köök
kitchen

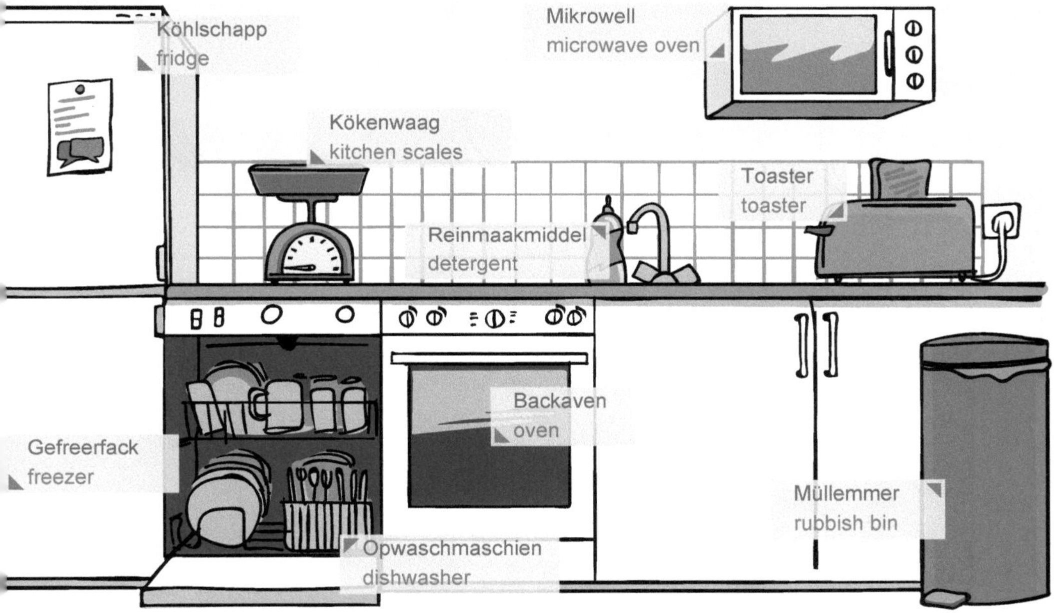
Köhlschapp
fridge
Mikrowell
microwave oven
Kökenwaag
kitchen scales
Toaster
toaster
Reinmaakmiddel
detergent
Backaven
oven
Gefreerfack
freezer
Müllemmer
rubbish bin
Opwaschmaschien
dishwasher

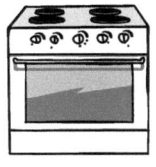

Heerd
cooker

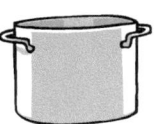

Pott
pot

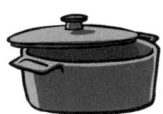

Gussiesern Putt
cast-iron pot

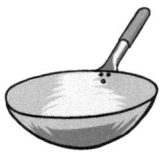

Wok / Kadai
wok / kadai

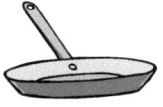

Pann
pan

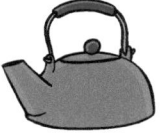

Waterkaker
kettle

Dampkaakputt

steamer

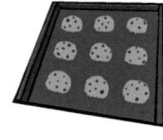

Backblick

baking tray

Geschirr

crockery

Beker

mug

Schaal

bowl

Eetsticken

chopsticks

Suppenkell

ladle

Pannenwenner

spatula

Sneebessen

whisk

Kaakseef

strainer

Seef

sieve

Riev

grater

Mörser

mortar

Grill

barbecue

Füerstell

open fire

Sniedbrett

chopping board

Nudelholt

rolling pin

Proppentrecker

corkscrew

Doos

can

Dosenaapner

can opener

Pottlappen

pot holder

Waschbecken

sink

Böst

brush

Swamm

sponge

Mixer

blender

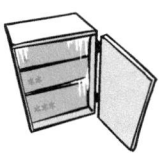

lesschapp

deep freezer

Nuckelbuddel

baby bottle

Waterhahn

tap

Köök - kitchen

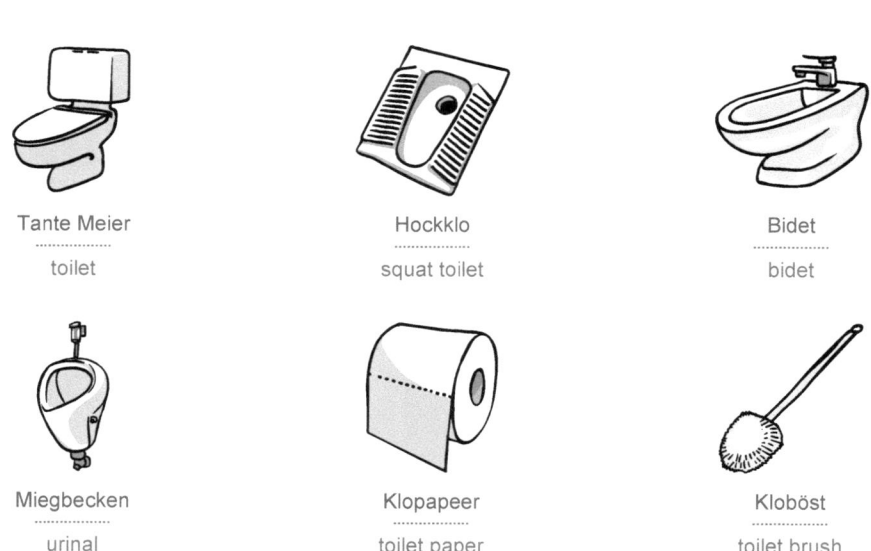

Baadstuuv

bathroom

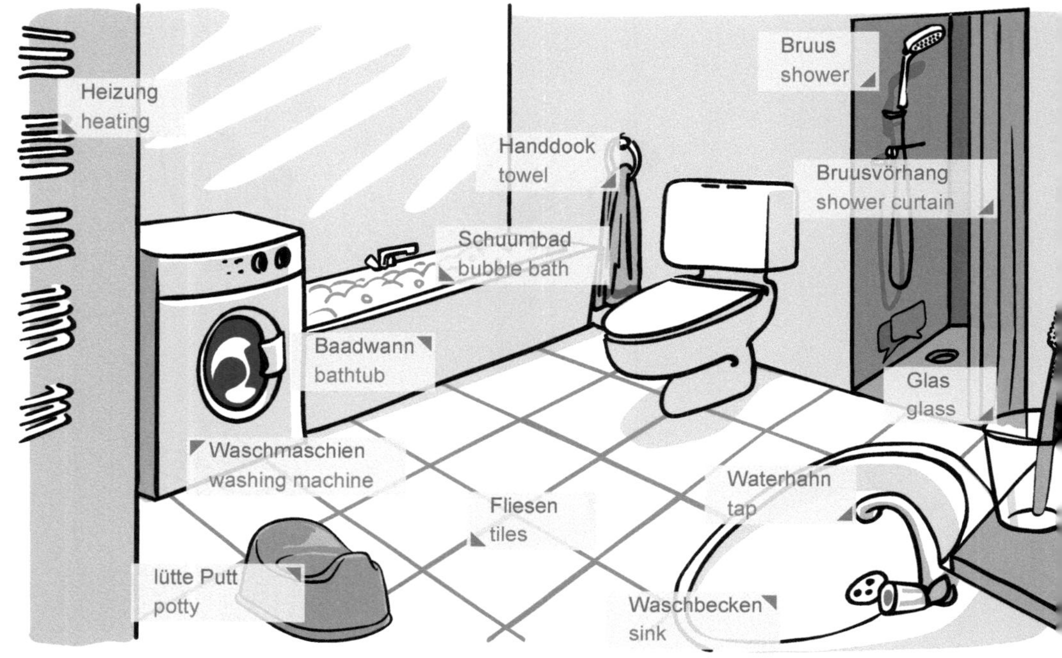

Heizung
heating
Handdook
towel
Bruus
shower
Bruusvörhang
shower curtain
Schuumbad
bubble bath
Baadwann
bathtub
Glas
glass
Waschmaschien
washing machine
Waterhahn
tap
Fliesen
tiles
lütte Putt
potty
Waschbecken
sink

Tante Meier

toilet

Hockklo

squat toilet

Bidet

bidet

Miegbecken

urinal

Klopapeer

toilet paper

Kloböst

toilet brush

Tähnböst

toothbrush

Tähnpast

toothpaste

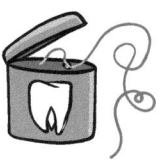

Tähnsied

dental floss

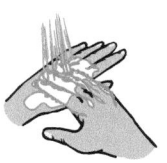

waschen

wash

Handbruus

handheld shower

Intimbruus

douche

Waschschöttel

basin

Rüchböst

back brush

Seep

soap

Bruusgeel

shower gel

Hoorwaschmiddel

shampoo

Waschlappen

flannel

Afloop

drain

Creme

cream

Deodorant

deodorant

Spegel

mirror

Kosmetikspegel

hand mirror

Raserer

razor

Raseerschuum

shaving foam

Raseerwater

aftershave

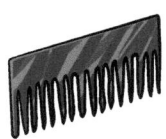

Kamm

comb

Böst

brush

Hoordröger

hair dryer

Hoorspray

hairspray

Smink

makeup

Lippensticken

lipstick

Nagellack

nail varnish

Watt

cotton wool

Nagelscheer

nail scissors

Rüükwater

perfume

Kulturbüdel

washbag

Schemel

stool

Waag

weighing scale

Baadmantel

bathrobe

Gummihanschen

rubber gloves

Tampon

tampon

Damenbinn

sanitary towel

Chemieklo

chemical toilet

Kinnerstuuv

child's room

Wecker
alarm clock
Knudeldeert
cuddly toy
Speeltüüchauto
toy car
Klöter
rattle
Poppenhuus
doll's house
Geschenk
present

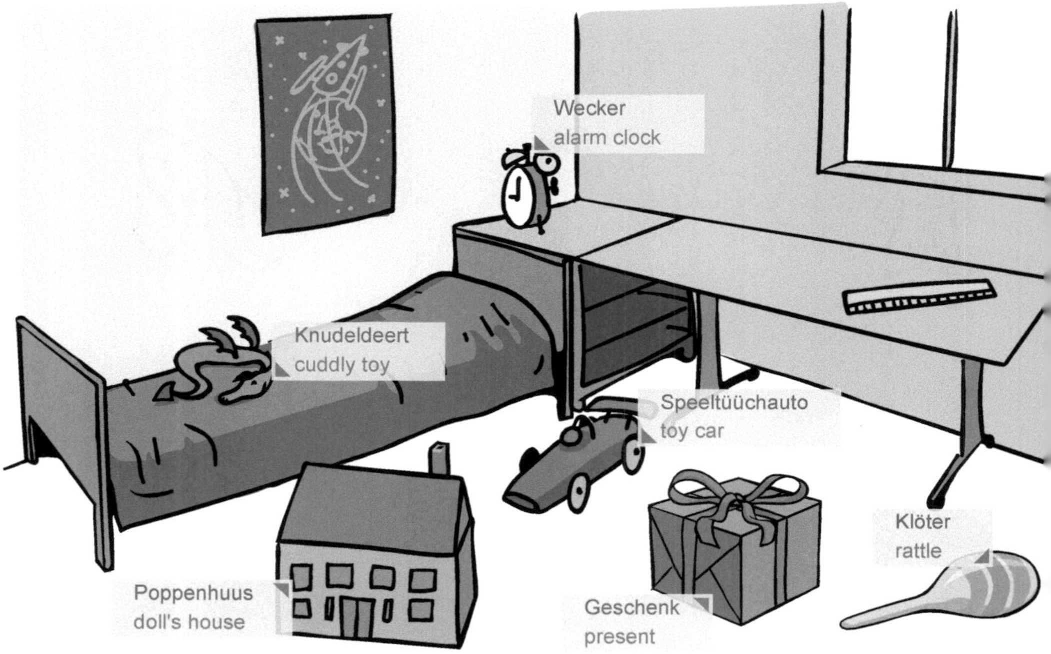

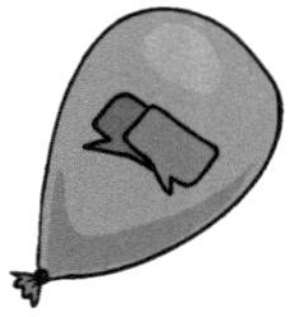

Luftballon

balloon

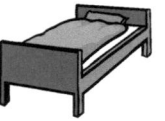

Puuch

bed

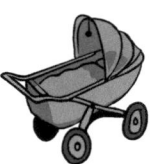

Kinnerwagen

pram

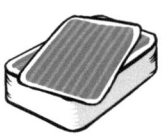

Koortenspeel

deck of cards

Puzzle

jigsaw

SUPER
MEGA

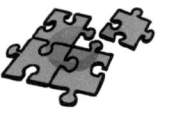

Billergeschicht

comic

Legostenen

lego bricks

Bustenen

building blocks

Action-Figur

action figure

Strampelantog

babygrow

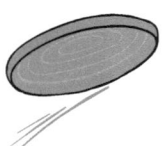

Frisbeeschiev

frisbee

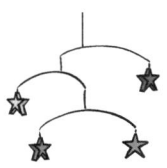

Mobile

mobile

Brettspeel

board game

Wörpel

dice

Modelliesenbahn

model train set

Snuller

dummy

Party

party

Billerbook

picture book

Ball

ball

Popp

doll

spelen

play

Sandkassen

sandpit

Schuckel

swing

Speeltüüch

toys

Speelkonsool

video game console

Dreerad

tricycle

Teddyboor

teddy bear

Klederschapp

wardrobe

Tüüch

clothing

Socken

socks

Strümp

stockings

Strumpbüx

tights

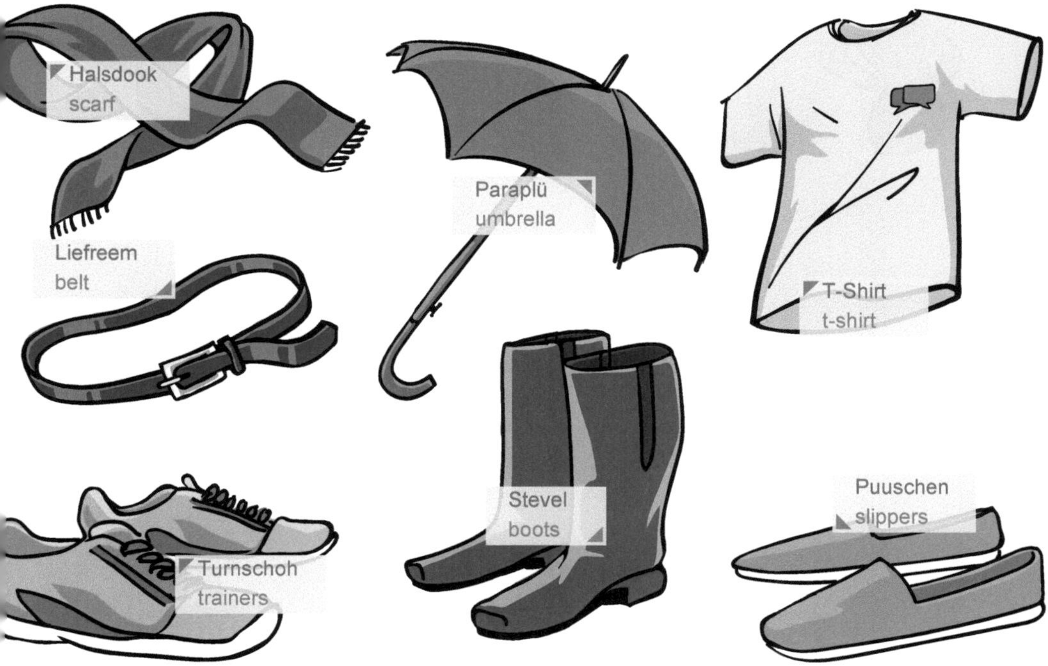

Halsdook
scarf

Paraplü
umbrella

T-Shirt
t-shirt

Liefreem
belt

Stevel
boots

Puuschen
slippers

Turnschoh
trainers

Sandalen
....
sandals

Schoh
....
shoes

Gummistevel
....
rubber boots

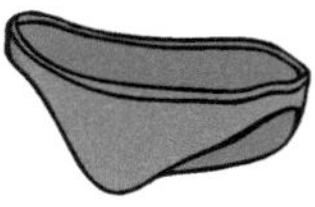

Ünnerbüx
....
underpants

Bostholler
....
bra

Ünnerhemd
....
vest

Lief

body

Büx

trousers

Jeansnüx

jeans

Rock

skirt

Bluus

blouse

Hemd

shirt

Pullover

pullover

Kapuzenpullover

hoodie

Blazer

blazer

Jack

jacket

Mantel

coat

Övertrecker

raincoat

Kostüm

costume

Kleed

dress

Hochtietskleed

wedding dress

Antog

suit

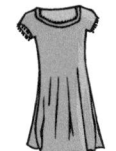

Nachtkleed

nightgown

Slaapantog

pyjamas

Sari

sari

Koppdook

headscarf

Turban

turban

Burka

burqa

Kaftan

kaftan

Abaya

abaya

Baadantog

swimsuit

Baadbüx

trunks

Korte Büx

shorts

Antog to'n Öven

tracksuit

Schört

apron

Handschoh

gloves

Knopp

button

Brill

glasses

Armband

bracelet

Halskeed

necklace

Ring

ring

Ohrbummel

earring

Mütz

cap

Klederbögel

coat hanger

Hoot

hat

Binner

tie

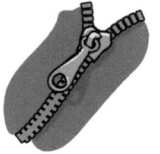

Rietslüter

zip

Helm

helmet

Drachtband

braces

Schooluniform

school uniform

Uniform

uniform

Severböten
....
bib

Snuller
....
dummy

Winnel
....
nappy

Büro

office

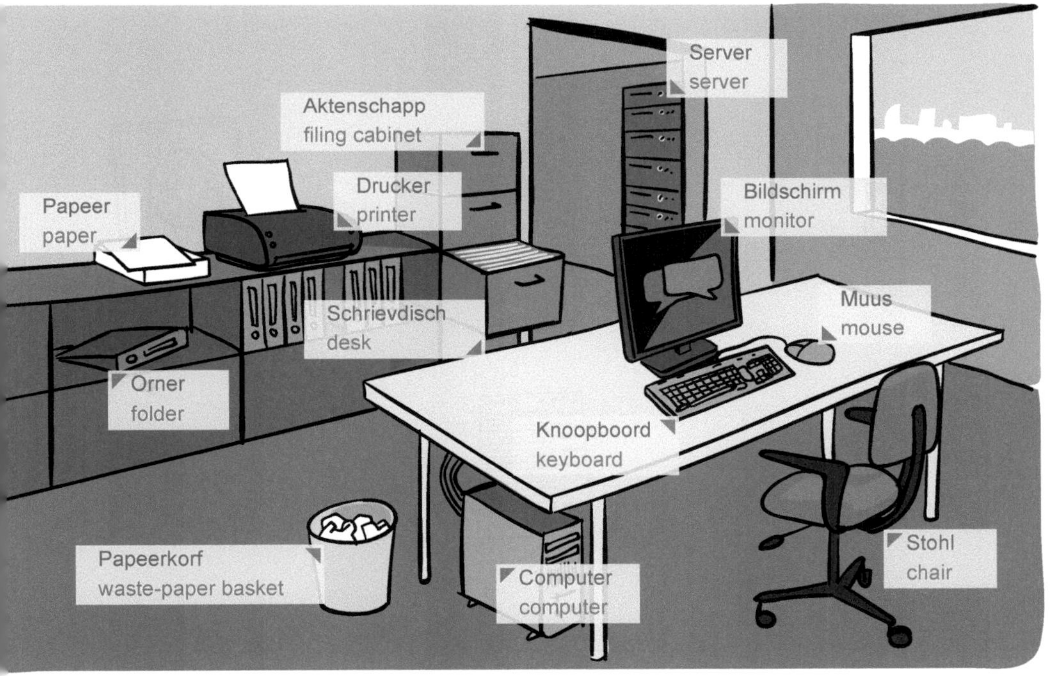

Server
server

Aktenschapp
filing cabinet

Drucker
printer

Papeer
paper

Bildschirm
monitor

Schrievdisch
desk

Muus
mouse

Orner
folder

Knoopboord
keyboard

Papeerkorf
waste-paper basket

Stohl
chair

Computer
computer

Koffiebeker
....
coffee mug

Taschenreekner
....
calculator

Internet
....
internet

Klappreekner

laptop

Breef

letter

Naricht

message

Ackersnacker

mobile

Nettwark

network

Kopeerapparat

photocopier

Software

software

Klöönkassen

telephone

Steekdoos

plug socket

Faxapparat

fax machine

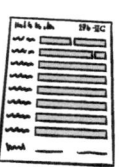

Formulor

form

Dokument

document

köpen

buy

betahlen

pay

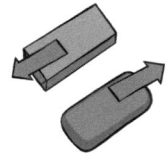

hanneln

trade

Geld

money

USD

Dollar

dollar

EUR

Euro

euro

JPY

Yen

yen

RUB

Ruvel

rouble

CHF

Swiezer Franken

Swiss franc

CNY

Renminbi Yuan

renminbi yuan

INR

Rupie

rupee

Geldautomat

cashpoint

Wesselstuuv

bureau de change

Gold

gold

Sülver

silver

Ööl

oil

Energie

energy

Pries

price

Verdrag

contract

Stüer

tax

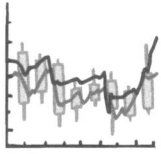

Andeelschien

stock

arbeiden

work

Anstellte

employee

Arbeitgever

employer

Fabrik

factory

Hökerie

shop

Profeschonen
occupations

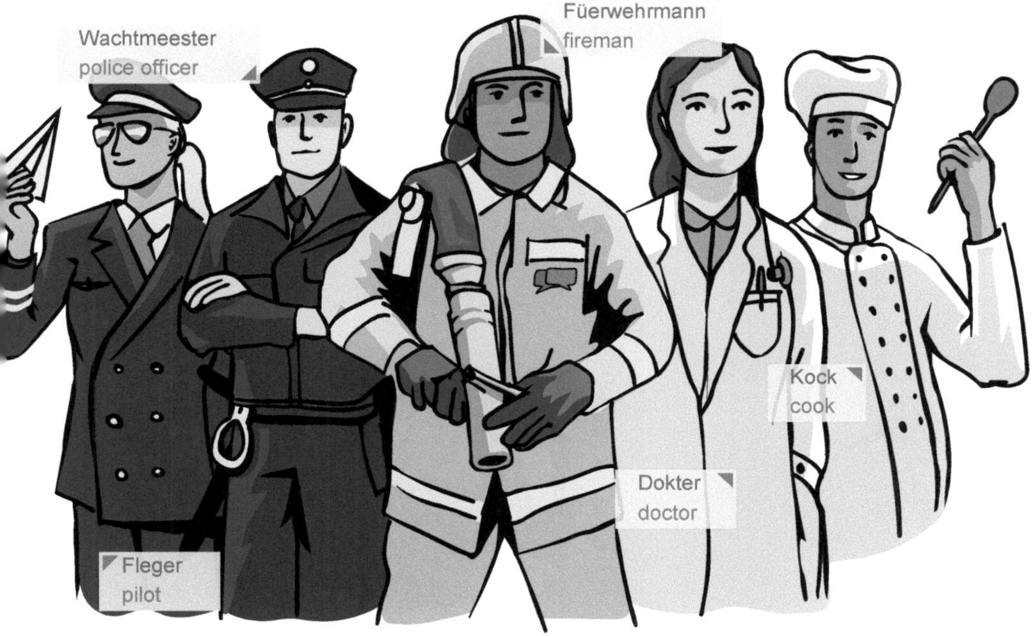

Wachtmeester
police officer
Füerwehrmann
fireman
Kock
cook
Dokter
doctor
Fleger
pilot

Goorner

gardener

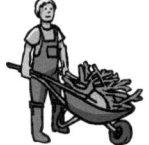

Discher

carpenter

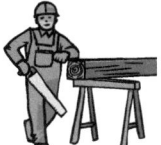

Neihersche

seamstress

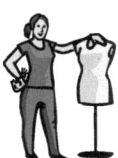

Richter

judge

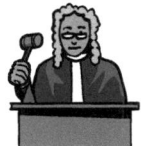

Chemiker

chemist

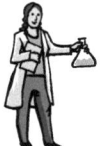

Schauspeler

actor

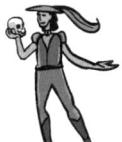

Busfohrer

bus driver

Taxifohrer

taxi driver

Fischer

fisherman

Reinmaakfru

cleaning lady

Dackdecker

roofer

Kellner

waiter

Jäger

hunter

Maler

painter

Bäcker

baker

Elektriker

electrician

Buarbeider

builder

Ingenieur

engineer

Slachter

butcher

Klempner

plumber

Postbüdel

postman

Suldat

soldier

Architekt

architect

Kasserer

cashier

Florist

florist

Putzbüdel

hairdresser

Schaffner

conductor

Mechaniker

mechanic

Kaptein

captain

Tähndokter

dentist

Wetenschopler

scientist

Rabbi

rabbi

Imam

imam

Mönk

monk

Paap

clergyman

Warktüüch

tools

Hamer
hammer
Tang
pliers
Schruvendreiher
screwdriver
Schruvenslötel
spanner
Taschenlamp
torch

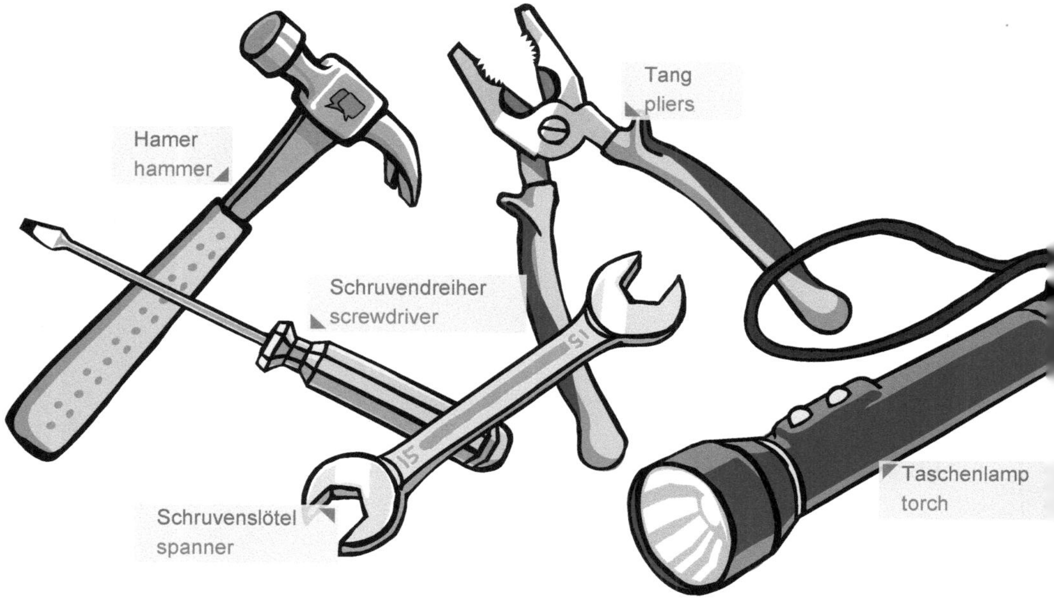

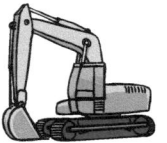

Grieper

digger

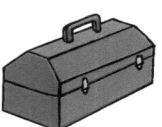

Warktüüchkassen

toolbox

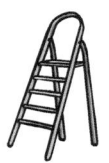

Ledder

ladder

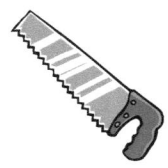

Saag

saw

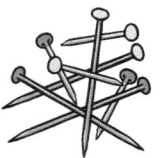

Nagels

nails

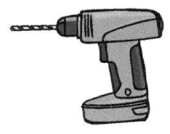

Bohrer

drill

heelmaken

repair

Schüffel

shovel

Schiet!

Damn!

Kehrblick

dustpan

Farvpott

paint pot

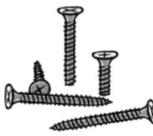

Schruven

screws

Musikinstrumenten
musical instruments

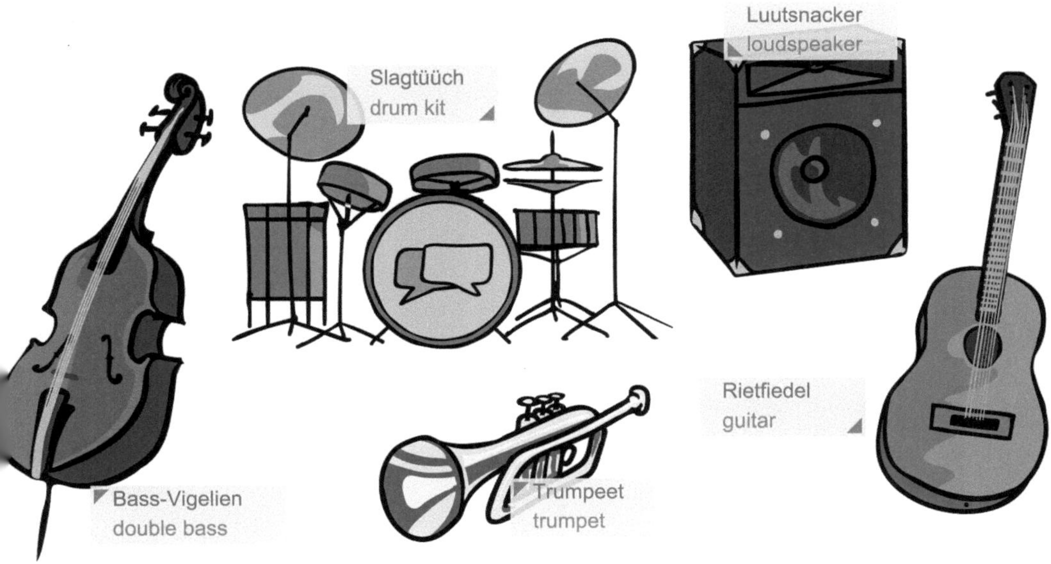

Luutsnacker
loudspeaker

Slagtüüch
drum kit

Rietfiedel
guitar

Bass-Vigelien
double bass

Trumpeet
trumpet

Klaveer

piano

Vigelien

violin

Bass

bass

Pauk

timpani

Trummeln

drums

Keyboard

keyboard

Saxophon

saxophone

Fleut

flute

Mikrofoon

microphone

Musikinstrumenten - musical instruments

Deertenpark

zoo

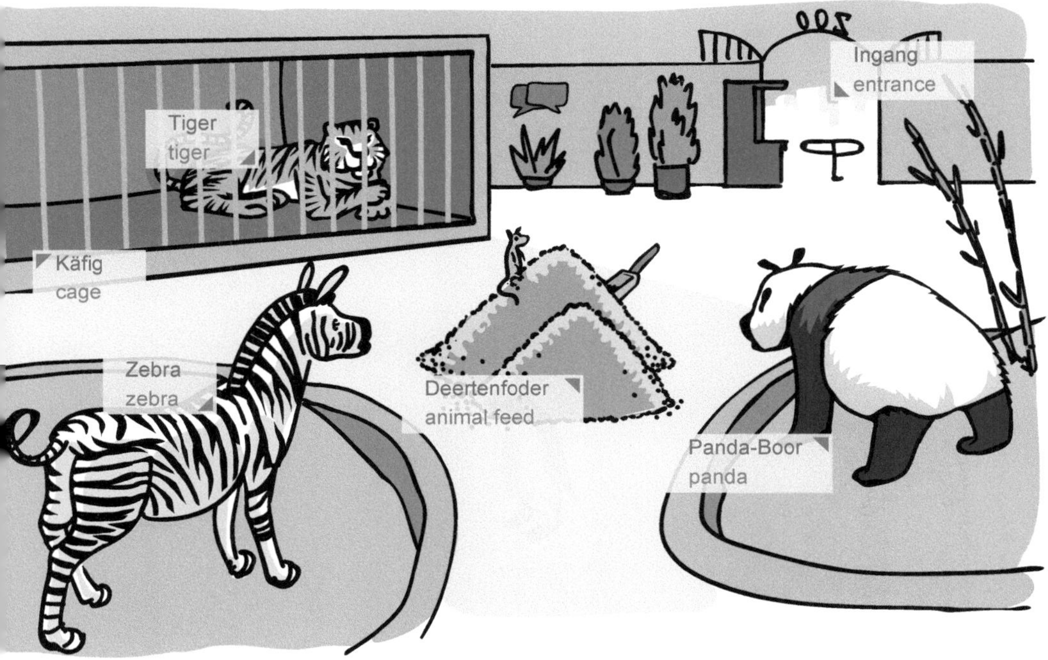
zoo
Ingang
entrance
Tiger
tiger
Käfig
cage
Zebra
zebra
Deertenfoder
animal feed
Panda-Boor
panda

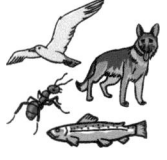

Deerten

animals

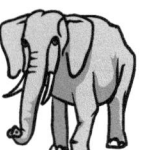

Elefant

elephant

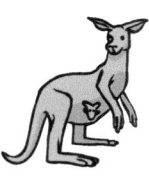

Känguru

kangaroo

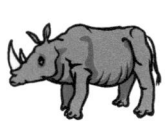

Neeshoorn

rhino

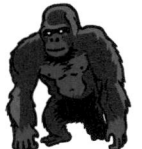

Gorilla

gorilla

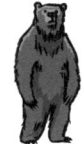

Boor

bear

Kameel

camel

Struuß

ostrich

Lööv

lion

Aap

monkey

Flamingo

flamingo

Papagoi

parrot

Iesboor

polar bear

Pinguin

penguin

Haifisch

shark

Pageluun

peacock

Slang

snake

Krokodil

crocodile

Oppasser in'n Deertenpark

zookeeper

Saalhund

seal

Jaguor

jaguar

Pony

pony

Leopard

leopard

Nilpeerd

hippo

Giraff

giraffe

Aadler

eagle

Wildswien

boar

Fisch

fish

Schildkrööt

turtle

Walross

walrus

Voss

fox

Gazell

gazelle

Amerikaansch Football
American football

Radfohren
cycling

Tennis
tennis

Korfball
basketball

Swümmen
swimming

Boxen
boxing

Ieshockey
ice hockey

Football
football

Fedderball
badminton

Leichtathletik
athletics

Handball
handball

Skilopen
skiing

Polo
polo

Aktivitäten
activities

lachen
laugh
springen
jump
ümarmen
hug
gahn
walk
singen
sing
drömen
dream
beden
pray
snuteln
kiss

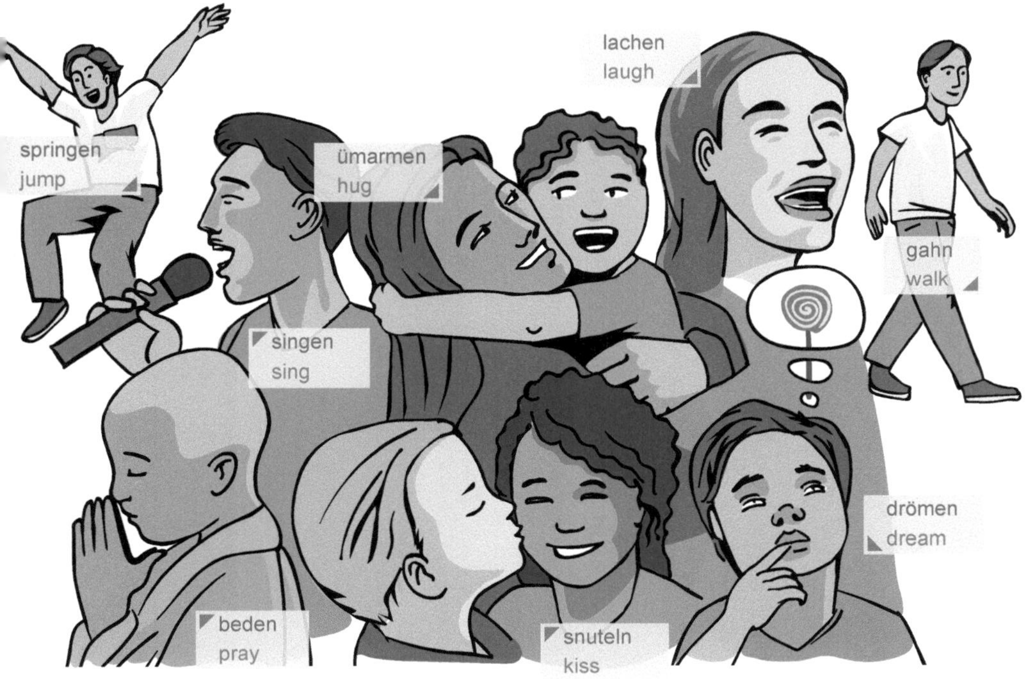

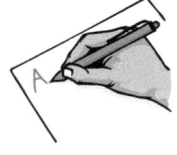

schrieven

write

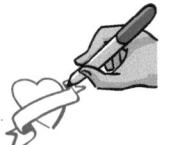

teken

draw

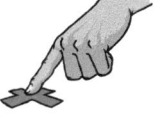

wiesen

show

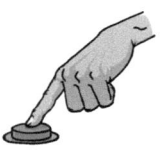

drücken

push

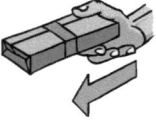

geven

give

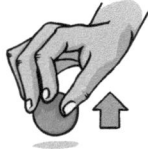

nehmen

take

hebben

have

doon

do

sien

be

stahn

stand

lopen

run

trecken

pull

smieten

throw

fallen

fall

liggen

lie

töven

wait

dregen

carry

sitten

sit

antrecken

get dressed

slapen

sleep

opwaken

wake up

ankieken

look at

wenen

cry

eien

stroke

kämmen

comb

snacken

talk

verstahn

understand

fragen

ask

hören

listen

drinken

drink

eten

eat

oprümen

tidy up

leefhebben

love

kaken

cook

fohren

drive

flegen

fly

Aktivitäten - activities

65

segeln

sail

reken

calculate

lesen

read

lehren

learn

arbeiden

work

de Plünnen tohoopsmieten

marry

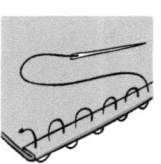

neihen

sew

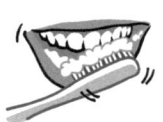

Tähnen putzen

brush teeth

dootmaken

kill

smöken

smoke

schicken

send

Familje
family

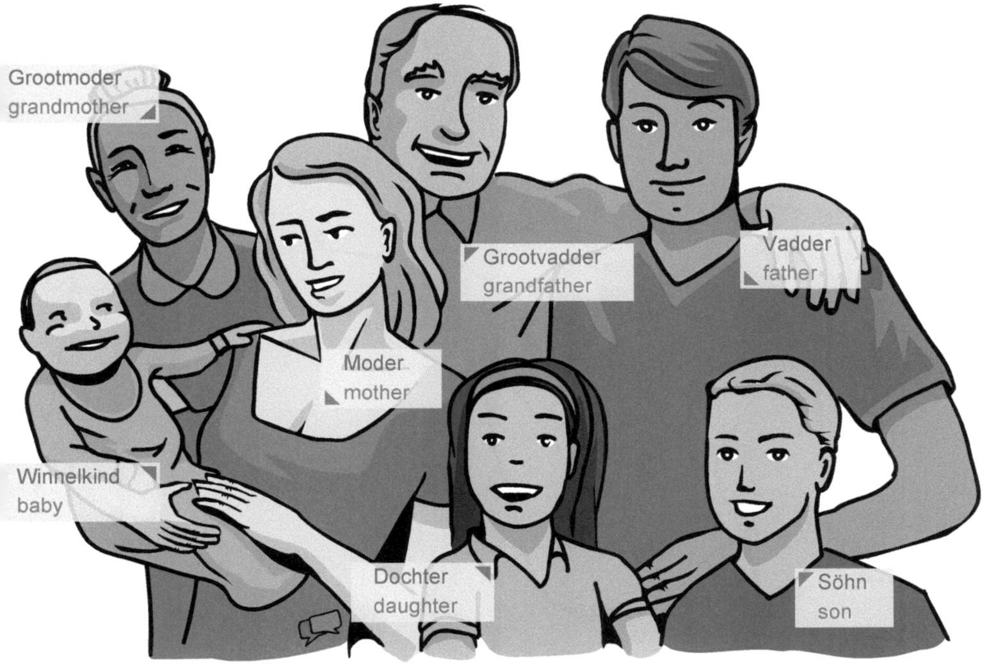
Grootmoder
grandmother
Grootvadder
grandfather
Vadder
father
Moder
mother
Winnelkind
baby
Dochter
daughter
Söhn
son

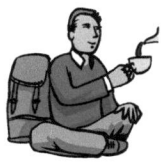

Gast

guest

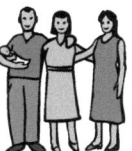

Tant

aunt

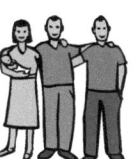

Unkel

uncle

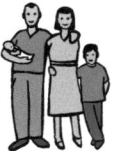

Broder

brother

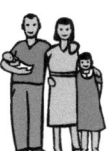

Süster

sister

Lief

body

Vörkopp
forehead
Oog
eye
Schuller
shoulder
Finger
finger
Gesicht
face
Kinn
chin
Hand
hand
Been
leg
Bost
breast
Arm
arm

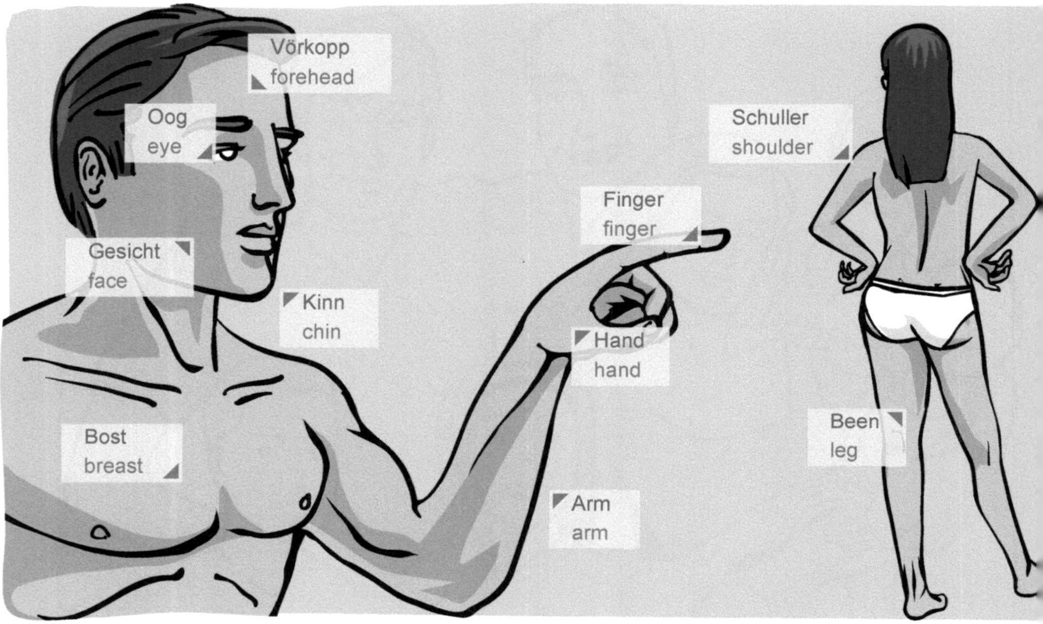

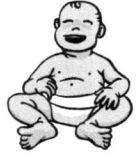

Winnelkind

baby

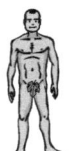

Mann

man

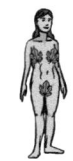

Fro

woman

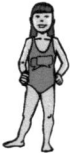

Deern

girl

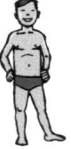

Jung

boy

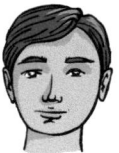

Arm

head

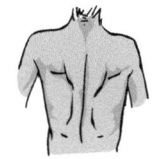

Rüch

back

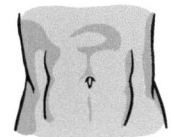

Buuk

belly

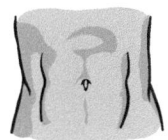

Navel

belly button

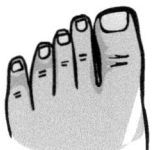

Teh

toe

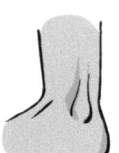

Hack

heel

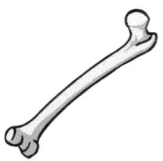

Knaken

bone

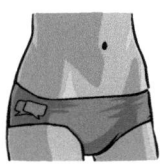

Hüft

hip

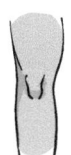

Knee

knee

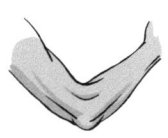

Ellbagen

elbow

Nees

nose

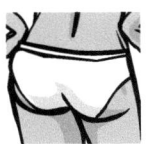

Achtersen

bottom

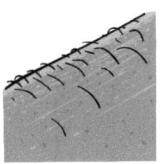

Huut

skin

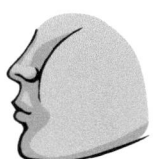

Back

cheek

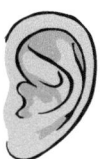

Ohr

ear

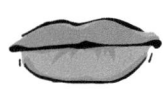

Lipp

lip

Mund

mouth

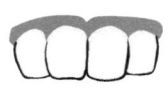

Tähn

tooth

Tung

tongue

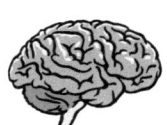

Bregen

brain

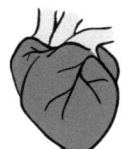

Hart

heart

Muskel

muscle

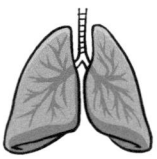

Lung

lung

Lever

liver

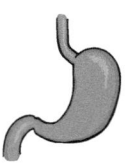

Maag

stomach

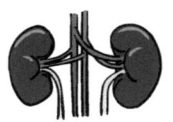

Neren

kidneys

Bislaap

sex

Kondoom

condom

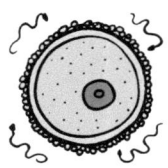

Eizell

ovum

Sperma

semen

Anner Ümstänn

pregnancy

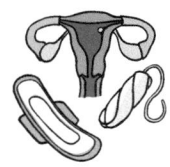

Menstruatschoon
....
menstruation

Scheed
....
vagina

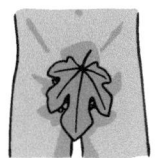

Pint
....
penis

Ogenbroe
....
eyebrow

Hoor
....
hair

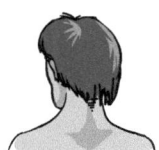

Hals
....
neck

Krankenhuus
hospital

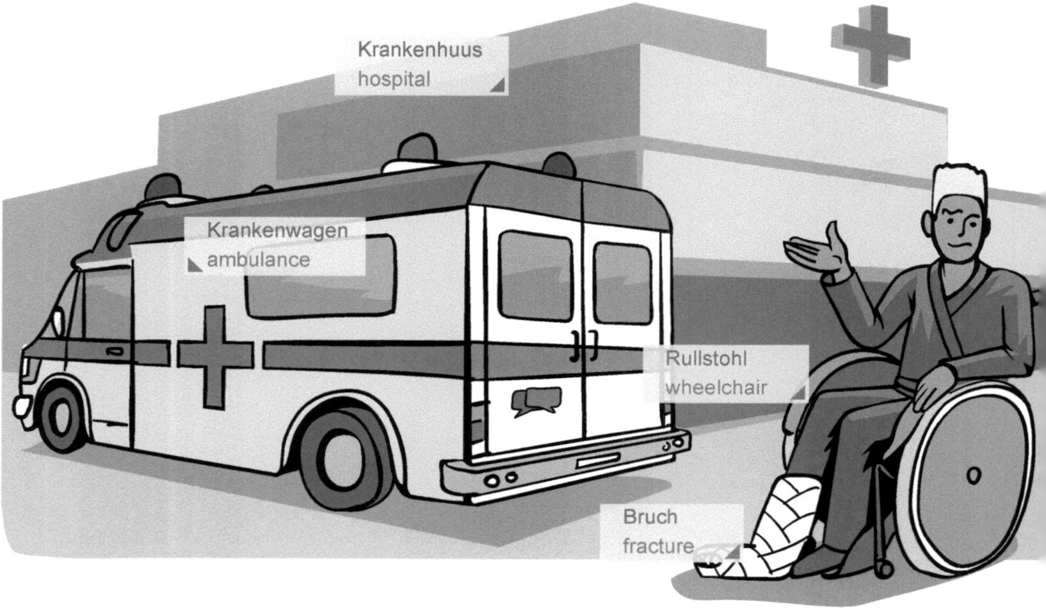

Krankenhuus
hospital
Krankenwagen
ambulance
Rullstohl
wheelchair
Bruch
fracture

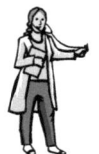

Dokter
doctor

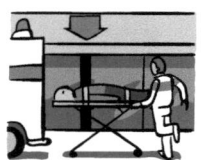

Nootopnahm
emergency room

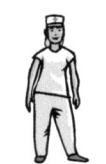

Krankensüster
nurse

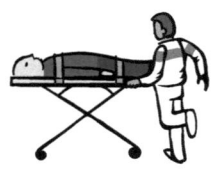

Nootfall
emergency

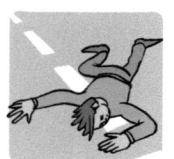

ahnmächtig
unconscious

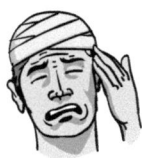

Wehdaag
pain

Verwunnen

injury

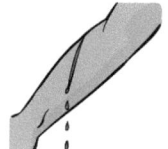

Blöden

bleeding

Hartinfarkt

heart attack

Slaganfall

stroke

Allergie

allergy

Hoosten

cough

Fever

fever

Gripp

flu

Dörchfall

diarrhoea

Koppwehdaag

headache

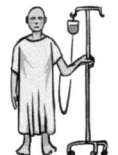

Kreeft

cancer

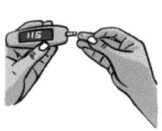

Zuckersüük

diabetes

Chirurg

surgeon

Chirurgsch Mess

scalpel

Operatschoon

operation

CT
CT

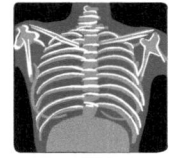

Dörchlüchten
x-ray

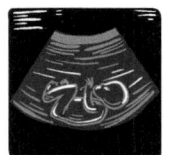

Ultraschall
ultrasound

Mask
face mask

Krankheit
disease

Töövruum
waiting room

Krück
crutch

Plaaster
plaster

Verband
bandage

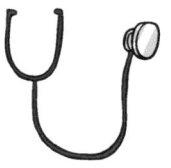

Insprütten
injection

Stethoskop
stethoscope

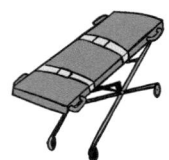

Draag
stretcher

Feverthermometer
clinical thermometer

Geboort
birth

Övergewicht
overweight

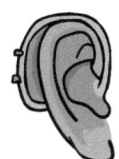

Höörapparat

hearing aid

Kiemfriemiddel

disinfectant

Ansteken

infection

Virus

virus

HIV / AIDS

HIV / AIDS

Heelmiddel

medicine

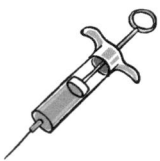

Impen

vaccination

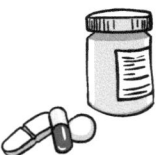

Tabletten

tablets

Pill

pill

Nootroop

emergency call

Blootdruck-Meter

blood pressure monitor

krank / gesund

ill / healthy

Hölp!	Alarm	Överfall
Help!	alarm	assault
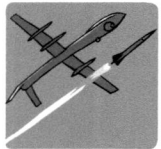		
Angreep	Gefohr	Nootutgang
attack	danger	emergency exit

Füer!	Füerlöscher	Unfall
Fire!	fire extinguisher	accident
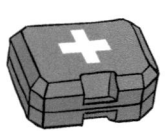		
Noothölpkoffer	SOS	Polizei
first-aid kit	SOS	police

Europa

Europe

Noordamerika

North America

Süüdamerika

South America

Afrika

Africa

Asien

Asia

Australien

Australia

Atlantik

Atlantic

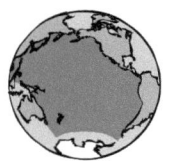

Pazifik

Pacific

Indisch Weltmeer

Indian Ocean

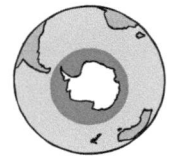

Antarktisch Weltmeer

Antarctic Ocean

Arktisch Weltmeer

Arctic Ocean

Noordpol

North Pole

Süüdpol
South Pole

Antarktis
Antarctica

Eerd
Earth

Land
land

See
sea

Eiland
island

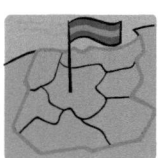

Natschoon
nation

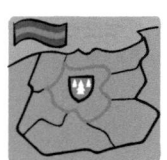

Staat
state

Tallenblatt

clock face

Stunnenwieser

hour hand

Minutenwieser

minute hand

Sekunnenwieser

second hand

Wo laat is dat?

What time is it?

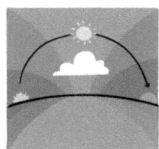

Dag

day

Tiet

time

nu

now

digetaalsch Klock

digital watch

Minuut

minute

Stunn

hour

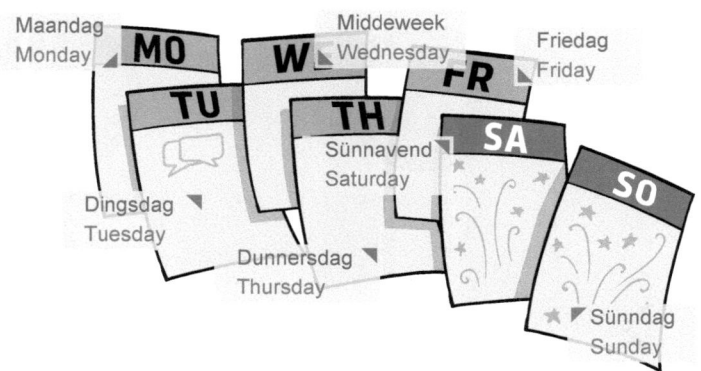

Maandag / Monday
Middeweek / Wednesday
Friedag / Friday
Dingsdag / Tuesday
Sünnavend / Saturday
Dunnersdag / Thursday
Sünndag / Sunday

güstern

yesterday

hüüt

today

morgen

tomorrow

Morgen

morning

Meddag

noon

Avend

evening

Arbeitsdaag

business days

Wekenenn

weekend

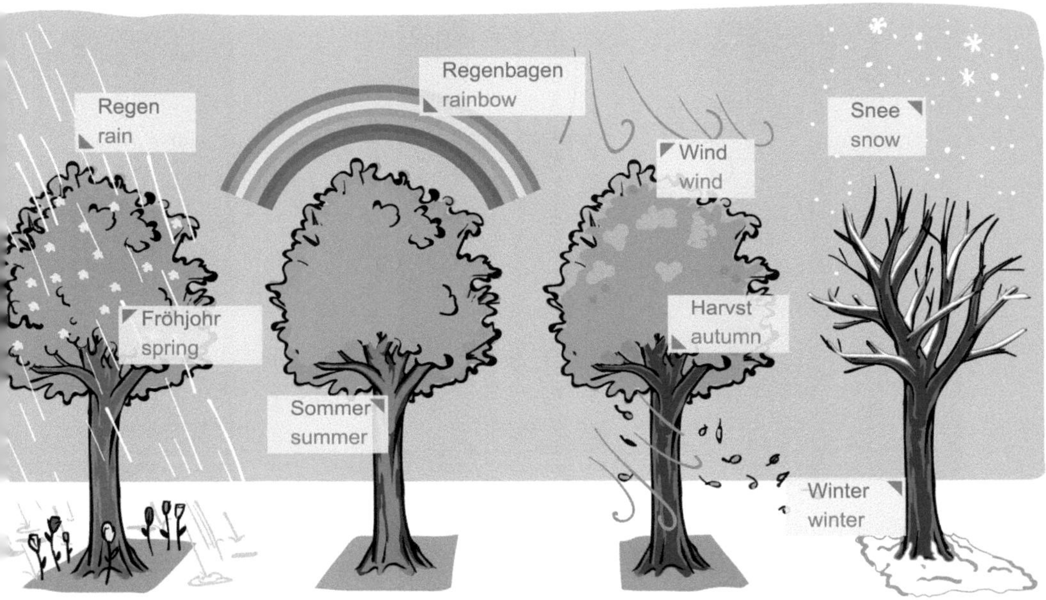

Regen
rain
Regenbagen
rainbow
Wind
wind
Snee
snow
Fröhjohr
spring
Harvst
autumn
Sommer
summer
Winter
winter

4.APRIL 11°
5.APRIL 4°
6.APRIL 13°
7.APRIL 8°
8.APRIL 10°

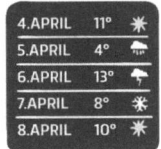

Wedervörhersaag

weather forecast

F
C

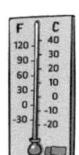

Thermometer

thermometer

Sünnenschien

sunshine

Wulk

cloud

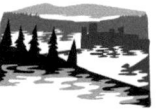

Nevel

fog

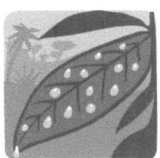

Luftfuchtigkeit

humidity

Blitz

lightning

Dunner

thunder

Storm

storm

Hagel

hail

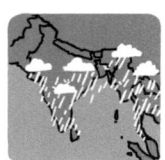

Monsun

monsoon

Floot

flood

Ies

ice

Januormaand

January

Februormaand

February

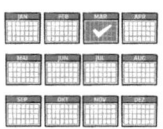

Martmaand

March

Aprilmaand

April

Maimaand

May

Junimaand

June

Julimaand

July

Augustmaand

August

Johr - year

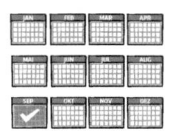

Septembermaand

September

Oktobermaand

October

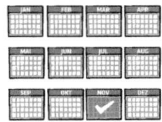

Novembermaand

November

Dezembermaand

December

Formen
shapes

Krink

circle

Quadrat

square

Rechteck

rectangle

Dreeeck

triangle

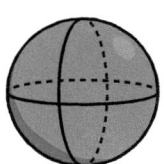

Kugel

sphere

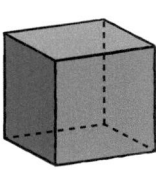

Wörpel

cube

Farven
colours

witt

white

geel

yellow

orangsch

orange

pink

pink

root

red

lila

purple

blau

blue

gröön

green

bruun

brown

gries

grey

swart

black

veel / wenig

a lot / a little

böös / verdreeglich

angry / calm

smuck / mies

beautiful / ugly

Begünn / Enn

beginning / end

groot / lütt

big / small

hell / düüster

bright / dark

Broder / Süster

brother / sister

schier / schietig

clean / dirty

kumpleet / nich kumpleet

complete / incomplete

Dag / Nacht

day / night

doot / lebennig

dead / alive

breet / small

wide / narrow

geneetbor / nich geneetbor

edible / inedible

böös / fründlich

evil / kind

fickerig / langwielt

excited / bored

dick / dünn

fat / thin

toeerst / toletzt

first / last

Fründ / Fiend

friend / enemy

vull / leddig

full / empty

hart / week

hard / soft

swoor / licht

heavy / light

Smacht / Döst

hunger / thirst

krank / gesund

ill / healthy

nich na't Recht / na't Recht

illegal / legal

klook / dummerhaftig

intelligent / stupid

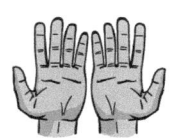

linkerhand / rechterhand

left / right

neeg / feern

near / far

nieg / bruukt
new / used

nix / wat
nothing / something

oolt / jung
old / young

an / ut
on / off

apen / slaten
open / closed

lies / luut
quiet / loud

riek / arm
rich / poor

richtig / verkehrt
right / wrong

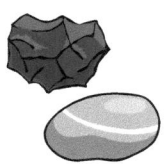

ruug / glatt
rough / smooth

trurig / glücklich
sad / happy

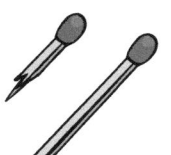

kort / lang
short / long

suutje / flink
slow / fast

natt / dröög
wet / dry

warm / köhl
warm / cool

Krieg / Freden
war / peace

0

null

zero

1

een

one

2

twee

two

3

dree

three

4

veer

four

5

fief

five

6

söss

six

7

söven

seven

8

acht

eight

9

negen

nine

10

teihn

ten

11

ölven

eleven

12

twölf

twelve

13

dörteihn

thirteen

14

veerteihn

fourteen

15

föffteihn

fifteen

16

sössteihn

sixteen

17

söventeihn

seventeen

18

achtteihn

eighteen

19

negenteihn

nineteen

20

twintig

twenty

100

hunnert

hundred

1.000

dusend

thousand

1.000.000

million

million

Engelsch

English

Amerikaansch Engelsch

American English

Chineesch Mandarin

Chinese Mandarin

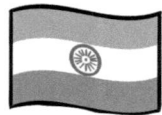

Hindi

Hindi

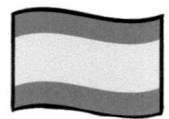

Spaansch

Spanish

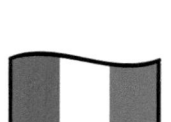

Franzöösch

French

Araabsch

Arabic

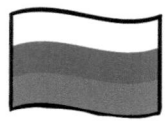

Rusch

Russian

Portugiesch

Portuguese

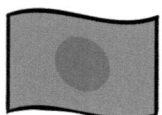

Bengaalsch

Bengali

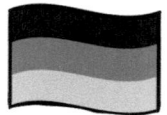

Düütsch

German

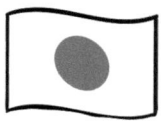

Japaansch

Japanese

ik
I

du
you

he / se / dat
he / she / it

wi
we

ji
you

se
they

keen?
who?

wat?
what?

woans?
how?

woneem?
where?

wannehr?
when?

Naam
name

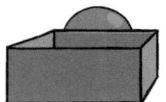

achter

behind

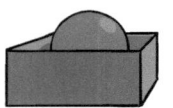

in

in

vör

in front of

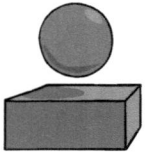

över

over

op

on

ünner

under

blangen

beside

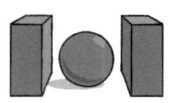

twüschen

between

Oort

place